IMAGES
of America

PALATINE
ILLINOIS

This sign, located at major entrances to Palatine, greets visitors to the village. It represents family, tradition, government, business, and culture. The structures depicted are, from left to right, the 1898 Patten House; the Municipal Center; The Harris Bank Building, the tallest building in Palatine, and the George Clayson House Museum.

IMAGES
of America

PALATINE
ILLINOIS

Palatine Historical Society

ARCADIA
PUBLISHING

Published by Arcadia Publishing
Charleston, South Carolina

Library of Congress Catalog Card Number: 2008937359

For all general information contact Arcadia Publishing at:
Telephone 843-853-2070
Fax 843-853-0044
E-mail sales@arcadiapublishing.com
For customer service and orders:
Toll-Free 1-888-313-2665

Visit us on the Internet at www.arcadiapublishing.com

This map indicates the development of the Village of Palatine within its original boundaries in 1887, with blocks, streets, and home plots laid out. Some of the land was still being farmed.

CONTENTS

ACKNOWLEDGMENTS

For the Palatine Historical Society, Alice Rosenberg and Marilyn Pedersen selected the photographs and did the research on them. The text was written by Alice Rosenberg, edited by Nancy Cairns and Beverly Keagle, and checked for accuracy by Marilyn Pedersen and Frank Regan. The "Tuesday Toilers" added their comments.

The following publications of the Palatine Historical Society were invaluable: *Hillside Cemetery* by Connie Rawa, *Palatine 1929* by Joan Murray, and *Palatine 1866-1991, 125 Years, Centennial Book Edition Updated*, a project of the Quasquicentennial Book Committee. We made extensive use of four notebooks of family histories compiled by the late Florence Smith Parkhurst, a lifelong resident of Palatine, a past president of the historical society, and an invaluable resource.

We thank the many donors who have gifted the historical society with photographs, postcards, and extensive archival material. We are always grateful for the devoted volunteers who have developed the Palatine Historical Society and keep it working. Marilyn Pedersen, museum coordinator and its only professional employee, began as a volunteer. She possesses tremendous knowledge of the history of the Village of Palatine. She is the backbone of this organization and can be counted on far beyond what might be expected.

—Alice Rosenberg, Archivist

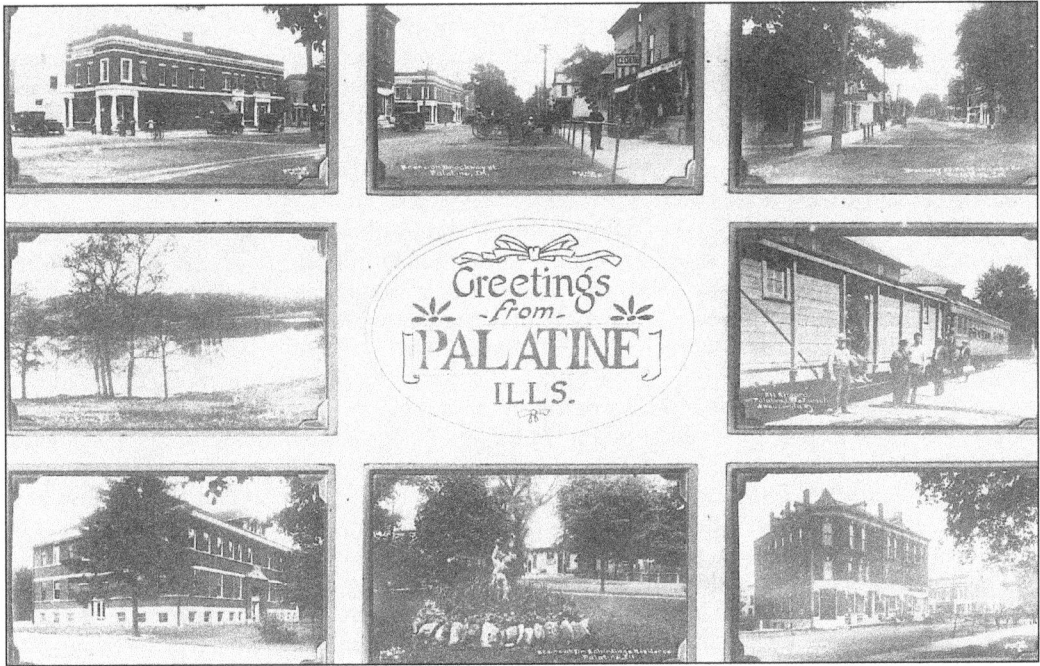

INTRODUCTION

The history of the development of the Village of Palatine in Palatine Township, Cook County, Illinois, began in 1810 when an error by a surveyor located the Wisconsin/Illinois boundary 50 miles south of the intended line. Illinois became a state in 1818. Cook County was formed in 1831. In 1850, the Illinois legislature passed an act compelling each numbered township to choose a name for identification purposes. It is said that the principal men of Township 42 met in a schoolhouse. Many names were considered, but "Palatine," the suggestion of Harrison Cook, prevailed. It was a fairly well established fact that Mr. Cook came from Palatine Bridge, New York.

The territory comprising Palatine Township in the northwest part of Cook County was largely prairie dotted with several prominent groves: Deer Grove in the northwest, Englishman's Grove to the west, Plum Grove to the south, and Highland Grove in the southwest. The gently rolling countryside and the cool shade of wooded groves seemed like home to the newcomers who had left green hills and fertile valleys to travel west. In general, the first settlers came from New York and New England. Relatives back home were sent for, and little settlements grew up in the four wooded tracts of the township. Early settlers discovered that this area had been an important American Indian center. Stories told to the settlers by the Potawatomis, who occasionally came this way to visit neighboring burial mounds, were substantiated by the trails and relics in the surrounding forests.

The first recorded history of a white man in the area dates to 1835, when George Ela settled in Deer Grove. Government land records indicate a claim was awarded to him in 1836. The first white child, born in 1838, was Clarinda Cady, whose parents had arrived in Deer Grove in 1837 from central New York State.

In 1853, plans began to extend the Illinois and Wisconsin Railroad (later the Chicago & Northwestern and then Union Pacific) west of Dunton Station (now Arlington Heights), and the railroad reached Palatine on June 10, 1855. The construction of a depot followed soon after. Service started with one freight train a day, and passenger service began in December 1855. Joel Wood, who had bought a farm in the vicinity of Palatine in February 1847, presumably owned the land north of present Palatine Road, and Elisha Pratt owned the land south of the street. They had the vision to see where the center of town would be located. Even one train a day meant several days saved in the marketing of merchandise. Joel Wood surveyed the village into lots, blocks, and streets in July 1855.

At first, there were post offices in both the north and south sections of the Township. After the location of the depot, a single post office was established in Palatine at D.B. Woods's store. Not everyone was so optimistic about the future of Palatine. Hiram Thurston is said to have laughed in Joel Wood's face when he offered him what is now the center of downtown Palatine for $10. It was a slough filled with cattails and green water.

The formation of Palatine as a village began on March 19, 1866, at a meeting of "resident" voters of Palatine Township to discuss whether to proceed with incorporation. At a meeting of voters held April 2, 1866, a vote resulted in 73 for and 20 against incorporation. Five residents and freeholders of the town were elected as trustees and one as police magistrate at another meeting on April 9th. The new trustees met the next day to elect Myron H. Lytle as president, and they appointed R.S. Williamson as clerk. The other trustees were Joel Wood, Henry Schirding, Solon M. Johnson, and F.G. Robinson. R.S. Williamson was police magistrate.

The town experienced a slow, steady growth, and the first development on a large scale started about 1920. In 1925, farms were selling for $400 an acre, a sewer system had just been completed, all streets had been or were being paved with reinforced concrete, and elaborate street lighting had been installed.

In the 133 years since the Village of Palatine was incorporated, numerous annexations have occurred, and many subdivisions have been built. Community services, which were rendered on a part-time or volunteer basis, have been expanded and staffed and operated by professionals. The small farm village located about 35 miles from the center of Chicago, out on the prairie, is now a Chicago suburb of 62,000.

One

THE PALATINE
HISTORICAL SOCIETY

The Palatine Historical Society had its beginning in 1955, when the Village of Palatine decided to throw a party and called it a "Centennial." The 100 years was based on Joel Wood's division of the area nearest the original depot into lots, blocks, and streets. The six-day celebration, sponsored by the Palatine Chamber of Commerce, culminated in a parade on July 10th. This Conestoga wagon boasts that W.R. Comfort and Sons was the oldest continuous business in Palatine. The lumber yard was located south of the tracks and west of Brockway Street until 1982, when it was demolished and replaced by what is now the Harris Bank. (A Quasquicentennial, 125 years, was held in 1966, based on the actual incorporation of the village.)

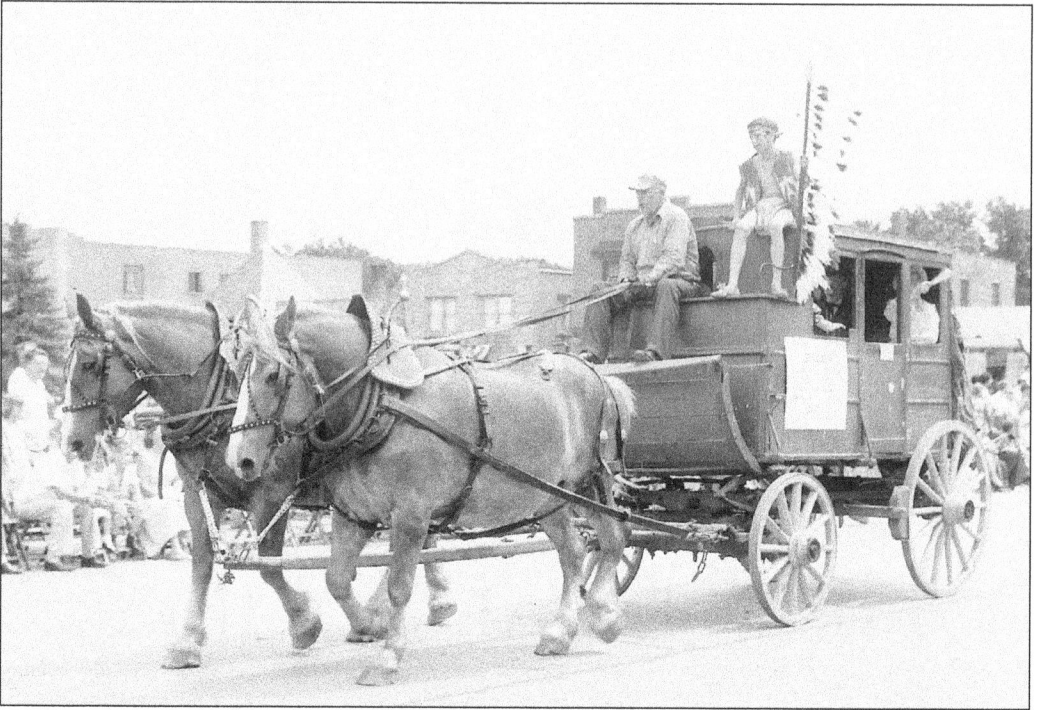

The old-time theme was typified by this stagecoach in the parade. The village of 4,000 was swelled by many outsiders who came to enjoy the festivities. The celebration also featured a ball, a carnival, a historical pageant, a pet parade, an alumni reception, street dancing, and a beard-growing contest.

The hand pumper in the parade had been purchased by the village volunteer fire company in 1887. Eventually, the pumper was sold to the Schaumburg Rural Fire Department. About 1941, it was purchased by Chicago auto dealer Carl W. Zepp, who restored it and loaned it to the Palatine Fire Department in 1949. In 1956, he gave them title to the equipment, which is now part of the historical society collection.

An editorial in the *Palatine Herald* by Stuart Paddock, a long-time Palatine resident, suggested that some organization help form a historical society. This prompted the Woman's Club of Palatine to convene a meeting on October 31, 1955, for that purpose. The Palatine Historical Society received its charter that year, with a membership of 67, and stated as its major function "the discovery and collection of material which would illustrate the history of the area." This house at 224 East Palatine Road became the home of the society in 1976. It had been built in 1873 by George H. Clayson, a nurseryman, who occupied it until 1880. The Wolf family, residents at the time, are pictured in front of the house in this photo, *c.* 1907.

Florence Smith Parkhurst holds the pen in this 1976 photograph of historical society members signing a contract for the purchase of Clayson House. Mrs. Parkhurst, a lifelong resident of Palatine and descendant of one of the original settler families in the village, was known as unofficial historian. She knew everyone, kept various types of records, and preserved artifacts, all of which she donated to the Palatine Historical Society. The library of the Clayson House Museum was named in her honor after her death in 1984. Others in the photo are, from left to right, Ann Oswald, Harry Benstein, Avery Wolfrum, Tom Ahern, and Roger Bjorvik. The Palatine Historical Society raised more than $200,000 to restore the house. The building is owned jointly by the Palatine Park District and the Palatine Public Library District. Funds for operation and maintenance are raised by tax levy by the Palatine Park District.

The Clayson house was occupied by many different people over the years and had been made into apartments. The original siding was covered, and the original roof was altered by the addition of a hip roof. The small porch on the east was removed and replaced by a screened-in porch.

Inside, the house was a mess. Many of the rooms were reconfigured to create the apartments. A restoration architect was retained to direct the return of the house to its original shape and condition. For instance, removal of a bathroom upstairs revealed the former existence of a rear stairway, which was then recreated.

13

Much of the restoration work was done professionally, but a great deal of the work was done by volunteers. In this photograph, the Palatine Jaycees are making the ornate outside trim in a workshop at Fremd High School. After the removal of the hip roof, they also hand cut new shingles. The original siding was uncovered and repaired, and the side porch was replaced.

Frank Regan and Marilyn Pedersen are seen in this photo, as volunteers, hanging wallpaper in the parlor of the house. Marilyn spent countless hours toiling as a volunteer to refurbish the interior. In 1986, she became an employee of the Palatine Park District with the title of Museum Coordinator and is still the only paid employee working in the museum.

The Clayson House has been fully restored and furnished as it was in the 1870 period. The historical society has developed collections that encompass the history of the area and of this Victorian period. Much of the material has been received through the generosity of former residents or their relatives. There are extensive artifacts, photographs, slides, maps, books, textiles, and other period pieces. Many persons have made use of these materials over the years. The society also continues to record and preserve more recent Palatine history. Docents conduct tours for school children, scouts, and other groups throughout the year. The historical society has developed a variety of slide programs that it presents to numerous organizations in the area.

Jan Loster, in period dress, is awaiting visitors to the annual Christmas open house in this December 1991, photo of the Clayson House, which is decorated as it might have appeared during the Civil War. Each year, a different theme is chosen for the holidays. The Clayson House, open to visitors on Tuesdays, Thursdays, and Sundays, is operated pursuant to a three-way agreement between the Palatine Public Library District, the Palatine Park District, and the Palatine Historical Society. Many volunteers work for the society to decorate the house, to serve as docents, and to raise money with projects such as a Victorian Dinner, a Cemetery Walk, a House Walk, and Victorian Teas. The society has published the following books: *Palatine 1929, A Slice of Life From the Good Old Days, Hillside Cemetery, Directory of Farmers in Palatine Township,* and *Palatine History 1866–1991.*

16

In 1980, Palatine Township wished to remove the 19th-century carriage house on its property. They offered it to the historical society if the society would pay the cost of moving it. Through financing and some donations, the society raised the $15,000. The moving project took one day.

Once the carriage house was in place, a modern garage at the side of the Clayson House, which had been used for storage, was removed. The exterior of the carriage house was painted. The society began a campaign to raise money to turn the building into a museum.

Preparing the Carriage House Museum was a long process. Almost $60,000 was raised. On the first floor, the building contains a Fire Museum which includes the 1887 hand pumper, the original 1887 fire bell, and other early fire paraphernalia. There is also an exhibit of early Palatine businesses. Since the Clayson House is not wheelchair accessible, a bathroom and an area in which to run a film showing the interior of the house has been provided. Upstairs, there is shelving and hanging space to store the society's many artifacts and textiles in a climate-controlled environment. The grand opening of the Palatine Deluge Fire Company Museum was held May 8, 1999.

Two

Rural to Commuter to Suburban

There were a number of mills of all kinds in Palatine during the latter part of the 19th century. This mill was probably owned by Ableman and Ost. There was a planing mill, to accommodate all the building that was occurring at the time, a lumberyard, a grist and flour mill, and a grain elevator. The property adjoined the railroad tracks west of Brockway, next to the Comfort grain elevator and lumber yard. The grain elevator was moved from the east side of Brockway, using the railroad tracks overnight when no trains were running. Farmers brought their grain and wheat from great distances, taking home ground feed for their animals and flour for their families.

PALATINE TOWNSHIP
AS OF 1835-1850
SHOWING
APPROXIMATE LOCATION OF 1ST CLAIM HOLDERS
AND THE
EXISTING ROADS-WATERCOURSES

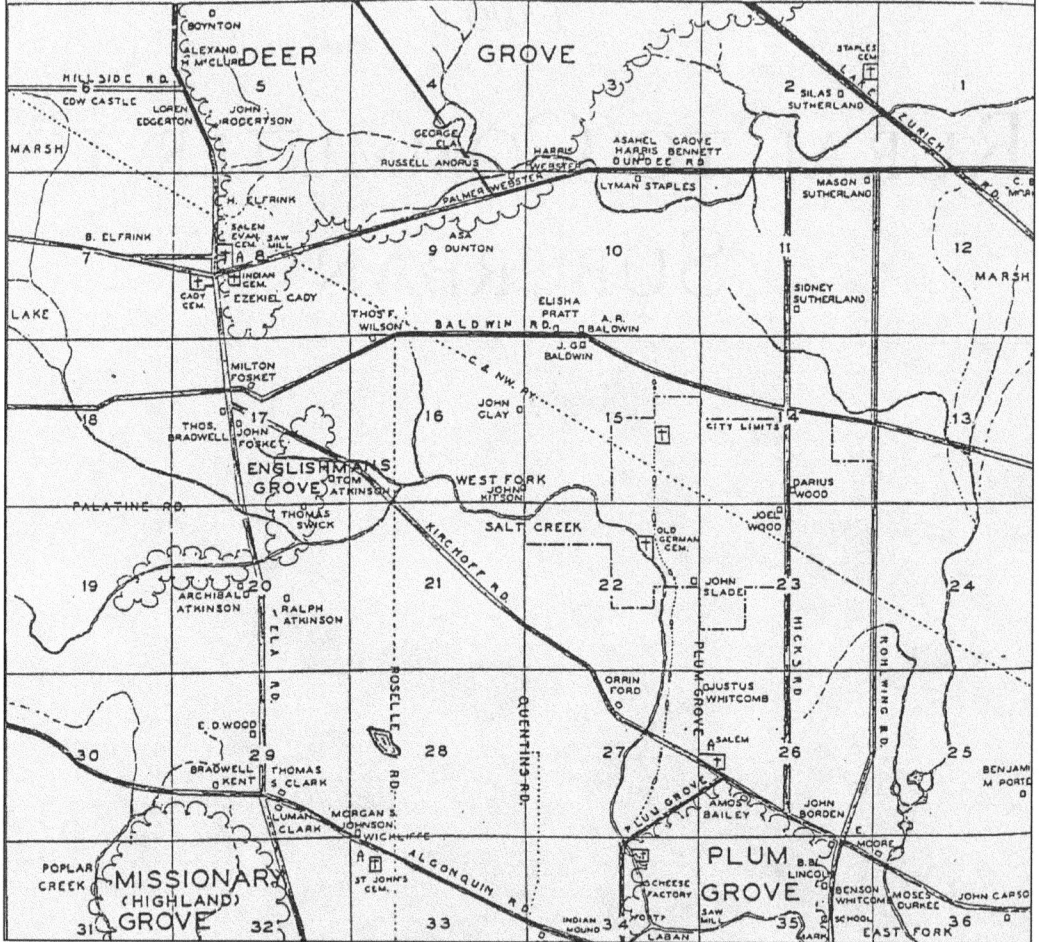

Trails made by the Americans Indians were invaluable to the first white inhabitants, and the "Indian Tree Trail Markers" led more than one worried traveler to the safety of his home. Every winding or diagonal road was probably originally an American-Indian trail. The American Indians were not governed by the surveyor's compass and made their way from one village to another by following the streams or the most convenient trails. Where the trail might be difficult to follow, they bent a sapling and fastened its upper end in the ground. As the sapling grew, it formed a peculiar "Z" that pointed the way to the next village or point of interest. Though the Village of Palatine did not exist in 1850, its outline is shown here. Also, some of the road name designations shown here did not exist in 1850.

The last time American Indians were seen in a group in Palatine was September 24, 1920. Chiefs from surrounding states, representing all the tribes that formerly roamed Illinois, pitched their tents in Deer Grove. The date had been officially set aside as "American Indian Day." The American Indians held various ceremonies and dances for three days.

Chief Whitefeather

This stock farm, at the corner of Baldwin and Roselle Roads, contained four silos when it was owned by Thomas Wilson. It was subsequently headquarters for Palatine builder Arthur T. McIntosh. He acquired farms in this area and developed housing, giving the area the name Inverness after his clan home in Scotland. In 1962, Inverness incorporated as a village. The four silos have been a landmark in Palatine Township for many years.

Road to Town,
Palatine, Ill.
18521

This postcard photo, *c.* 1900, shows Hicks Road, which was northeast of the village. As late as a 1925 map shows, this area was not included within the village limits. The carriage is heading south into town. A golf course was later located to the west and replaced by an office complex. The east side of the road was developed into a shopping center.

A Bit of Nature along Nason Creek,
Palatine, Ill.
18523

Nason's Creek ran under Hicks Road (and still does) where the bridge is in the above photograph. In recent years, the area under the bridge has been excavated to accommodate the Palatine Bicycle Trail, so riders would not have to cross Hicks Road, a major four-lane street into town that is now within the city limits.

Although the post office was located in the Village of Palatine, it served the entire Palatine Township. Most of the residents lived outside the village limits. In this picture, the postman poses with his U.S. mail wagon. He would hitch it to a horse and deliver mail throughout the township.

This Jahnke Mill stood on the south side of Sherman between Benton and Fremont in what is now a residential area. This mill held the most fascination for children because it was operated by wind. It stood on a barren knoll on a dead-end street. When a good strong wind arose from any direction, the big sails would go "lickety split." The Jahnkes operated the mill from 1879 to 1894.

The Haemkers moved many buildings and houses during the early days of Palatine. It was much simpler in the village before the advent of electricity because there were no overhead wires crossing the streets. It is evident here that a very large steam tractor was used. There is also a policeman present. It was the Haemkers who moved the grain elevator down the railroad tracks when the building was too wide for the streets. The family continued to move Palatine buildings for many years, including moving the carriage house, which became the Carriage House Museum, from Plum Grove Road to the site of the Clayson House on Palatine Road in 1980.

This was the Schrader Gravel pit that was only about 2 blocks south of the main part of town. The company has posed here with all their equipment and employees. The area is now entirely residential.

This farmer has probably come into town to take some grain to one of the mills. His horses and wagon are sitting in the center of town, south of the railroad tracks. The depot is to his right, the Comfort Building is in the center, and the Batterman brick building is to the left.

In addition to the train, Palatine did have a form of transportation service. For 10¢, this "Palatine Buss" carried passengers to nearby Deer Grove Park, a private park which drew people from as far away as Chicago. The Chicago and Northwestern Railroad would carry them to the stop at Palatine, where this "buss" would take them the rest of the way. When the Palatine, Lake Zurich, & Wauconda Railroad was formed, it made the same trip to the park, but in much less time.

Picket fences, lovely houses, and plank sidewalks were now common in Palatine, although it was still pretty much a rural community. Frank John and Mary Schutter Theis are enjoying a ride through town in their sporty little buggy.

This railroad park was in the center of town. The tracks are to the right. Looking west is the Comfort grain elevator across Brockway Street. The park has long since disappeared.

This is the first Palatine depot, built c. 1855 by Hiram Thurston. The site and lumber were both given by Joel Wood. The depot was placed on the north side of the tracks between Brockway and Bothwell Streets and was used until 1948. The first railroad, the Illinois and Wisconsin, failed, and the stockholders lost everything. A new company was formed, and the name changed to Prairie du Chein and Fond du Lac. In 1859, this railroad was taken over by the Chicago and Northwestern Railroad. The Northwestern was unique among American railroads. It was left-handed. Purchase of the original engines from England was one of the reasons suggested for this.

John Arps and William Brockway are working inside the original depot. When the railroad came to Palatine in 1855, it provided a much quicker way for this farm community to transport its products to market. Passenger service also increased. The railroad now made it possible for commuters to live in the country, Palatine, and work in the City of Chicago.

In 1948, Bothwell Street was closed to vehicular traffic, and this new station was built on the Bothwell Street crossing. The earlier depot was razed. In the 1970s, a new station combined with shops replaced it at a location a few blocks west. Presently, plans are underway to construct a fourth depot east of Smith Street and north of the tracks.

In 1905, the Palatine Village Board had granted a franchise creating the Palatine, Lake Zurich, & Wauconda Railroad. It had been subscribed to by local people, who believed there was a real need for a railroad that would connect Lake Zurich & Wauconda with the outside world via Palatine. This photo of the Sunday, September 6, 1911, grand opening shows that it was a gala affair. Thirty-six hours earlier, there had been no engine, no cars, and the road bed had been unfit for the transportation of passengers. Local residents had volunteered to shovel cinders onto the road bed. By opening day, the road had been completed only a little north of Dundee Road. The public walked the rest of the way into Deer Grove Park.

"All Aboard" on Palatine, Lake Zurich & Wauconda Ry.

Brooks IP Photo

On Friday before the opening, the Northwestern Railroad sold the new company an engine and rented them a car. Thus, it was possible to celebrate Palatine Day at Deer Grove Park, which was a stop on the line. Thousands of people rode the line on weekends. The two passenger cars could not accommodate the crowds, so the overflow rode the freight box cars and hung onto the steps.

By present standards, the engine was not much to look at, but she stood for all the desires and dreams of the people who created this railroad. They named her "Maude," after the mule comic strip character that was popular at that time. By 1915, the railroad was in financial difficulty.

The increased use of this *c.* 1907 vehicle and motorized trucks led to the demise of the Palatine, Lake Zurich, & Wauconda Railroad. The Northwestern did not take the road over, as some had hoped, and it was dissolved in 1920. The rails were later taken up and sold for scrap during World War II (WWII).

This "filling station" was located on Northwest Highway, south of Lincoln. This was a typical sight in the 1920s and later. The operator apparently lived next door to his business. The advent of the automobile and facilities such as this created the beginning of Palatine as a suburb. People were now able to live in one place and "drive" to their work. Mike's Bike Shop now occupies this site.

In this 1929 aerial of downtown Palatine, it can be seen that the streets have been paved, a step taken in 1924. Bothwell Street at the railroad is still open. The 1928 high school building does not appear in this photo but was located just below this view on the left. The Batterman brick building looms over the rest of town. The unfinished stores in the lower right corner remained that way for years. Eventually, business buildings were erected and a Jewel Food Store was located there, followed by an S&H Redemption Center. The space is now occupied by Mia Cucina Restaurant.

This Tesmer family cottage was located in the privately owned Deer Grove Park. When the Cook County Forest Preserve District made this their first park in 1915, some of the houses were moved to the Gainer Park (across from Deer Grove) and Teonia Woods (south of Kirchoff Road and east of Plum Grove Road) subdivisions. This early 1930s photo shows Carol and Bob Tesmer near the cottages in Gainer Park.

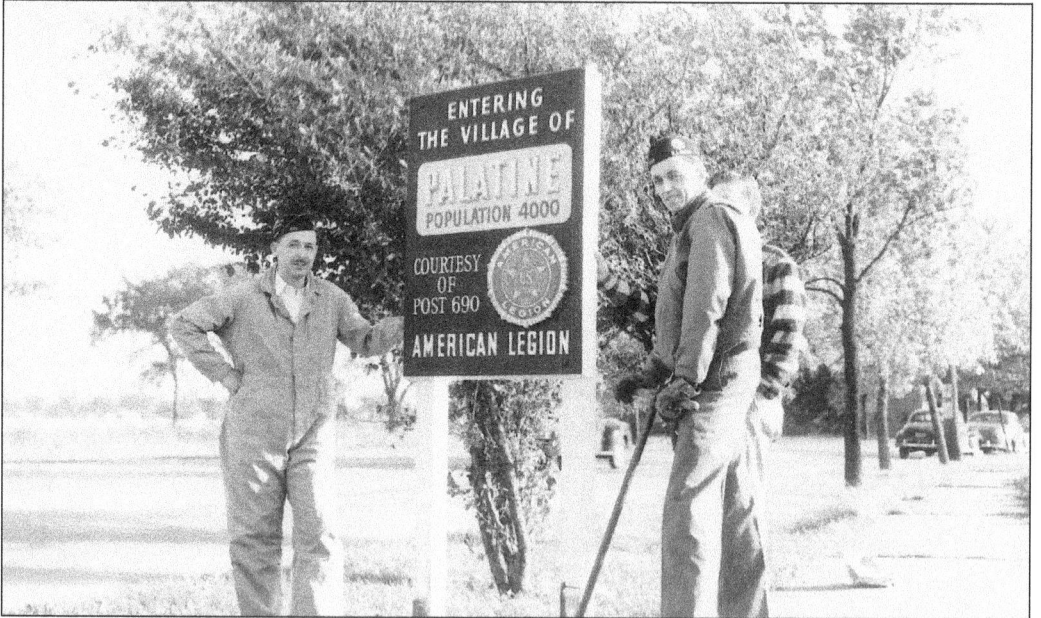

This sign was built and proudly displayed by the Palatine American Legion in 1950. This was almost double the population of 10 years earlier and about four times that of 30 years before. There had been growth, but it was slow. After 1950, in the post-WWII years, the population began to explode.

Three

PUBLIC INSTITUTIONS

In 1883, there were 1,011 children enrolled in school from nine districts in Palatine Township. George C. Whipple, the first school trustee, was elected in 1869. There is no photo of the first town school in District 15 (c. 1860), but it was a one-story frame building on Wood Street, probably on land donated by Joel Wood. This is a photo of a kindergarten class in the early 1900s. It is believed that Rose Converse Starck operated a kindergarten at her home on the northwest corner of Colfax and Plum Grove Streets. It is very possible that the public schools did not offer kindergarten. The Converse family lived on a farm near Palatine and moved into town in 1855. In 1908, Rose married Rufus Starck, and they purchased the Converse home.

In 1869, this two-story frame building, containing four rooms and a basement, was constructed on the site of the original school. Three young people constituted the first graduating class in 1877. In 1883, approximately 200 students attended school in this building. An addition on the north side in 1888 added two rooms to the facility.

Eventually, the school population outgrew the wooden facility. A brick building was erected on the enlarged site in 1912. The school was named Joel Wood School but has always been called the Wood Street School. The building was razed in 1979, and Victorian-style houses that blended into this residential neighborhood were built. Consolidated School District 15 was formed in 1946, and, in the next 50 years, 20 new schools were constructed.

There are many school class photos in the historical society collection. All the first and second-grade students in this 1909 class at the Joel Wood School have been identified. The teacher is Margaret Young. There are more photos from this year and quite a few of 1913–1914 classes. Many class photos have been recorded on postcards.

When Charles F. Cutting was principal of District 15 from 1875 to 1880, he founded the high school department, which occupied one room upstairs in the wooden school. In this photo, the high school was located on the top floor of the brick Joel Wood School. After leaving Palatine, Judge Cutting continued as attorney for the high school, and, in 1929, he donated $1,000 for library books for the high school.

A $125,000 bond issue to build a high school passed in 1926. Land on Wood Street, two blocks east of the present school, was purchased for $13,375. The facility housed up to 300 students. A theater on the west side was named Cutting Hall. A matching projection on the east housed a gymnasium. On opening day in 1928, there were 125 students. The faculty consisted of a principal and seven teachers.

In this 1952–1953 addition, an academic section, cafeteria, new gymnasium, music department, and shop areas were added. Another addition in 1969 increased the capacity. However, it became necessary to build a new Palatine High School in 1977 in the northeast section of town. All of the 1928 building, except Cutting Hall, was razed. The two additions which remained are shared by the village hall and the Park Department.

Walter Sneible, pictured in a workshop with his brother George, was the janitor at the brick Joel Wood School for 41 years. Walter had assisted his father, Michael, who had served as janitor for 10 years. Walter assumed the position at his father's death in 1917. The brothers' grandfather, John, had come to the Palatine area in 1868.

Construction of a connected system of sewers began in 1919. In this photo, a horse-drawn wagon and a large steam engine are shown being used to lay the sewer pipes. The project was held up several years because of litigation and contention. The administration was swept out of office, and the village was divided along political lines. Eventually, the sewer was completed, and Palatine became one happy family again.

The members of this Palatine Village Board of Trustees in the 1890s are, from left to right, as follows: (front row) Ernest Prellberg, Albert Olms, and Isaac Kuebler; (back row) Mr. Sigwalt, Rush Putnam, Charles Ost Sr., Mr. Horstman, and John Bergman. Albert Olms was board president in 1893 and again from 1899 to 1908.

This first village hall on Slade Street was opened in 1899. It was used for board meetings, political meetings, and entertainment. The building also served as a fire station with a bell in the tower to call the volunteer firemen. Later, it became the site of the first fire station separate from the village hall. Currently, it is occupied by offices and some shops.

At an 1897 citizens meeting, a petition was presented to build a water works for $15,000, a pump standpipe for $9,500, and a building for $6,970. This water works building stood at 100 South Brockway Street and later became the site of the second Palatine Municipal Building. The standpipe was erected on Colfax Street.

This imposing structure replaced the original village hall in 1930. The Municipal Building contained two stalls for fire equipment. Village offices and the police department were located in the building until an adjoining structure on Washington Street was built in 1964 for the police. The building was razed after all village operations were moved to the former Palatine High School on Wood Street. Tamarack Senior Residence now occupies the site.

On July 7, 1877, the Deluge Fire Company was organized. It numbered 45 men, all of them volunteers. One brick and two wooden cisterns were constructed to provide water. In 1887, a hand pump and a fire bell were purchased. Both of these items are owned by the Palatine Historical Society and form the nucleus of the Carriage House Fire Museum. Firemen of the 1896 company are shown here.

Until the purchase of the pump, the fire equipment consisted of a four-wheel cart and this hose cart. The volunteer firemen here are posed in front of the original village hall/fire station on Slade Street. With the installation of water mains in 1897, the fire department was reorganized, and firemen were paid 60 ¢ per drill. If they failed to attend a drill, they were fined 50 ¢.

This Municipal Building on Brockway provided only enough space for two fire trucks. The volunteer firemen were given permission to tear down the old village hall on Slade Street. There, they erected the first home of their own with room enough for all their equipment. With volunteer labor, the building cost only $8,500, entirely paid for by funds raised by the fire department.

The fire trucks in this 1948 photo are at the Slade Street Station. In 1953, the firemen expanded the facility. The second floor provided an auditorium available for public and private gatherings. The first full-time firefighter was hired in 1971. The first paramedics graduated in 1972. The last of the volunteers retired in 1984. The Slade Street Station was closed and sold in 1981 and now contains offices.

This was opening day in 1960 for the fire station at Colfax and Hale Streets, built on the site of the old standpipe. The department could now answer calls on both sides of the tracks without being delayed by trains. It was expanded in 1974 and dedicated to all the men who died in the line of duty. It is named for Orville Helms, the first full-time fire chief.

Providing police protection for Palatine had been an irregular process until Henry Law was hired in May 1896, as a full-time night watchman and lamplighter at $40 per month. He continued to serve until 1919, at which time he was receiving $80 per month. Henry Law sits here with his wife, Annie Witt Law. The photo was donated by Margaret Stroker Witt, a niece of the Laws.

Herman Schrader was appointed a special night watchman without salary in 1895, allowed $5 per month in 1897, rising to $40 per month in 1912. In 1913, he became a full-time, uniformed policeman when the board voted to hire two "police" for $55 per month, with said police to be in regulation uniform when on duty. Schrader and Henry Law continued to serve until 1919.

This 1950 Palatine Police Department consists of, from left to right, as follows: (front row) Officer Don Foxworthy (chief from 1956 to 1962), Officer Ray Bitz, and Parking Officer Bill Wolf; (back row) Officer Joe Yost, Chief Herb Moehling, and Lieutenant Frank Meyer (chief from 1951 to 1956). Four men served as chief until March 1973, when Jerry Bratcher came to head the department. He now serves as chief for a force of 96 policemen.

On September 8, 1923, the first Palatine Library opened in this small rented building at 3 North Bothwell Street. The collection of 300 books began as a Boy Scout project, which evolved into a citizens' committee that raised $1,000 and formed a temporary library board. A special election in 1923 established a library board and a library tax levy. A board was chosen at a regular election in 1925.

Lottie Hart was appointed as the first librarian. The facility was open Wednesdays and Saturdays from 3 p.m. to 5:30 p.m. and 7 p.m. to 9 p.m. Sixty-two borrowers registered the first day. In 1946, the library was moved to 55 West Wood Street. An open house was held there on October 6, 1948, to celebrate the 25th anniversary of the library and to honor Lottie Hart, who was still serving as librarian.

A bond issue for $125,000 was passed in 1957 to purchase the Ost property at the corner of Brockway and Wood Streets. The building was remodeled and enlarged. The new facility opened to the public on June 8, 1958. A new, larger library was erected on Benton Street in 1975. Once again, this facility was outgrown, and the present magnificent Palatine Public Library was built and occupied in 1992.

This first bookmobile was a bare trailer, outfitted with shelves, a librarian's desk, card files, and an oil burner. Dr. Noble J. Puffer of the Cook County School Board instituted this new project with the Palatine Library. During the first year of operation, 1936–1937, 14,393 books were circulated. The program was discontinued in 1941 because of the gas rationing created by WW II.

The Palatine Park District was formed after voters approved a bond issue of $75,000 on May 31, 1947, to purchase the site which is now known as Community Park. With the help of subscriptions and private gifts, the park site, ball field, and a recreation building were provided. The swimmer in this photo is helping to celebrate the opening of the first community pool on July 9, 1955.

Palatine Township acquired its first permanent home when this Schultz property, at 37 North Plum Grove Road, was rented in 1955. A resolution to purchase the property for $30,000 was passed in 1960. Behind the house was the building that would become the Palatine Historical Society's Carriage House Museum. In 1992, the township moved its administrative functions to the facility on South Quentin Road, which already housed their Senior Center.

Four

DOWNTOWN

In this *c.* 1890 photograph, we are standing in the street at the junction of Brockway and Slade Streets, looking west down Slade. Henry Matthei, wearing a vest and white shirt, is standing in front of his H.C. Matthei Store. He later moved his store to the corner of Bothwell and Slade Streets. This building was replaced by the Schoppe Store and became known as the Schoppe corner. The small building two doors down, next to the residence, was the original home of the *Palatine Enterprise*. Hosea C. Paddock came to town and purchased the newspaper in 1899. Later, he acquired the *Cook County Herald*, which was based in Arlington Heights. Both the paper and the family resided in Palatine for many years but eventually moved to Arlington Heights. Paddock Publications grew from a small weekly into a daily newspaper with multiple local editions covering the northwest, west, and southwest suburbs.

The Schoppe family came to the area in 1853 and were farmers. Two sons, Harry and Louis, opened a general store in 1892 and occupied the Brockway/Slade site from 1894 until 1967, a year after Harry Schoppe died. For a time, the Schoppes also operated a garage on South Brockway and sold automobiles.

Harry Schoppe stands behind the counter of his store in 1917. Louis Schoppe died in 1944. It was about then that Schoppe's stopped selling groceries. Old-timers used to gather around the pot-bellied stove for conversation and storytelling. The wooden building burned down while occupied by 26 North Mod Shop and was replaced by a modern brick building that now houses a card shop.

50

On the left is Kunze's Saloon, which stood on the southeast corner of Brockway and Slade Streets. Across Brockway is Schoppe's Store in this 1910 photo. Oswald Kunze emigrated to America in the 1880s and came to Palatine in 1904 to operate the saloon. He left for Texas in 1916 and sold the building to Dr. Carl Starck.

This was the Kunze saloon after Dr. Carl Adam Starck remodeled it into a hospital in 1916, then added to it in 1919. The hospital also trained nurses. Dr. Starck arrived in Palatine with his widowed mother in 1899. He closed the hospital in 1950 because of a shortage of nurses. Since then, the building has had a variety of tenants, including a drug store, Army recruitment center, and offices.

This is Brockway Street looking south from the tracks, c. 1900. The Batterman Brick Block is on the left (east). There is a watering fountain beside it, the top tier for horses and the bottom for dogs. Across Slade Street is Kunze's Saloon. On the right (west) are three stores, then the bandstand, with Schoppe's across Slade. The streets are still unpaved, and the sidewalks are wooden.

This is the same view of Brockway Street in the 1920s. The sidewalks are no longer wooden, and the streets are paved. On the right side, the bandstand at the end of the three stores has been replaced by the Palatine National Bank. You can still see Schoppe's across Slade Street. On the left, it is possible to see the old Kunze Saloon, now transformed into Dr. Starck's Hospital.

These are the three stores on the west side of Brockway in 1913. W.H. Brockway opened his hardware store with William Ost and bought him out in 1910. Mr. Toynton is standing in front of his drug store. On the Slade Street corner is Ike Blum's Tavern.

The men in front of Ike Blum's Tavern (west corner of Brockway Street and the tracks) are, from left to right, Isaac Blum, Christ Reuter, Ernie Lowe, and Sam Ryder. Peeking from the upstairs windows are Carl Blum and Mrs. Blum. Fred Kunze is on the bicycle. Isaac Blum was born in Palatine and raised in Arlington Heights. He returned to Palatine and purchased the tavern in 1900, operating it until 1917.

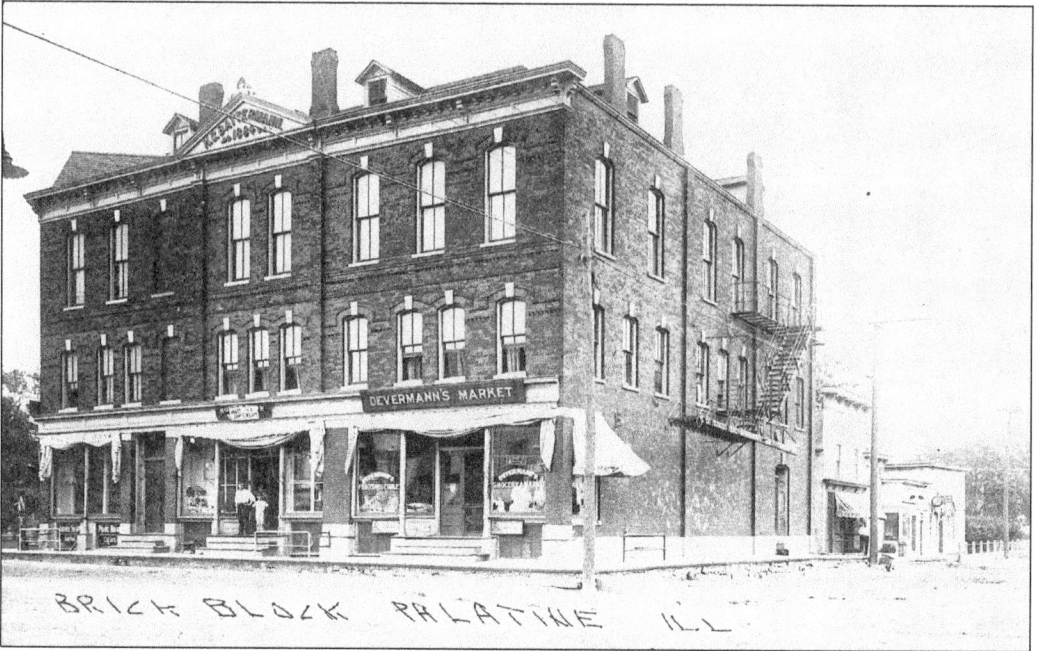

BRICK BLOCK PALATINE ILL

Henry C. Batterman built the Brick Block in the triangle formed by the railroad tracks and Slade Street on the east side of Brockway Street in 1884. It was the tallest building in Palatine and the pride of the village. The building contained stores at the street level and offices above. The top floor had a room for the Maennerchor and a hall known as the Opera Hall.

When Henry Batterman died in 1902, he left the Brick Block to his grandsons, Dr. William Abelman and Dr. Henry Abelman. The building was demolished in 1938, and the piece of land remained vacant for a number of years. Eventually, the bank that is now the First Bank & Trust Company of Illinois was erected on the site.

The Pahlman and Hans "Cheap Cash Store" was located on the southeast corner of the Batterman Brick Block. In this photo, Pahlman, Hans, and Ost are standing in the doorway. The Palatine Bank occupied the other corner of the building. The Palatine, Lake Zurich, & Wauconda Railroad had its first office on the corner of the second floor.

This same view of Brockway was taken a little south of the others in 1955. The Brick Block is gone, and the triangle is still vacant. The Palatine National Bank is on the right (west). South of Schoppe's Store are Zimmer Hardware, Schmidt Electric & T.V., and Al's Tavern on the corner. Some years later, all the parking meters were removed from downtown.

This photograph was taken *c.* 1920 of Brockway Street looking north from Chicago Avenue (Palatine Road) toward the tracks. On the right (east) are the Palatine Hospital and the Brick Block across Slade Street. On the left, there is the tavern on the corner. The sign adjacent to it is for the driveway to the Palatine Garage (Expert Repairing and Welding), which is behind the buildings.

Again, this is the east side of Brockway Street looking north from Chicago Avenue, probably a few years later. The car sits in front of Dede's Sweet Shop. Next is Henry Schlenker Auto and Electric Supplies. The Palatine Post Office and Illinois Bell Telephone are located on the first floor of the Starck Building. The hospital is on the second floor.

In this photo, we are again looking north on Brockway Street, this time from Slade Street with the Brick Block on the right (east). Note, however, the "firemen's light." When lit, it was supposed to call the volunteer firemen to duty.

This picture, c. 1930s, shows the west side of Brockway from Slade Street. The Palatine National Bank is on the corner. Next to it is National Tea Co. (groceries), Schroeder's Pharmacy, and Bockelman & Son Hardware. A bank (now Harris Bank) currently occupies this entire block. A street sign reading "Slade St." has been hung on the pole to the right.

Otto A. Schroeder stands in front of his drugstore at 40 N. Brockway on Christmas morning about 1935. The children shown with him were winners in a popularity contest held by this store at Christmastime.

On January 29, 1949, John Wilson opened the Ben Franklin Store at 36 North Brockway Street, the site of the former National Tea Co. The Wilson family had come to Palatine Township in 1838. While serving as a volunteer fireman, John Wilson died trying to save his store in 1973.

The Comfort family came to Palatine in 1858 to farm at Rohlwing and Baldwin Roads. In 1874, Wesley R. Comfort opened Comfort and Slade Grain and Lumber with his father-in-law, just south of the tracks on Brockway. In this 1930s photo, Wesley II and Clarence Comfort stand in front of their Lumber and Material Co. with employees. In 1968, what is now the Harris Bank was erected on this site.

The railroad water tower can be seen to the right of this grain elevator of the Comfort Co. The elevator was powered by a blindfolded horse traveling in a circle. Cups on belts scooped up the grain, which had been dumped from farmers' wagons, and threw it into a bin. When the market price was right, the grain was shipped to Chicago.

The location of this Bruhns Meat Market is believed to have been on the west side of Brockway, south of Slade Street. Later, Henry Bruhns moved the store. Standing in the doorway are, from left to right, John Foreman and Henry Bruhns.

Harry Schoppe sold farm implements and automobiles in this garage at 11 South Brockway Street. After WW II, Fred Korber Jr. occupied it as the Cork and Bottle Store, shown in this 1958 photo. Dobby Dobkin acquired it in 1963, added the former Palatine Post Office Building when it moved in 1971, and changed the name to World Wide Liquors. The Palatine Road corner was cleared for a parking lot.

This is Slade Street, east of Brockway just past Kunze's Saloon, in a picture taken before 1884. One of the men standing in front of Luerssen & Co. Wagon and Carriage Shop is Chris Schering. He had come to America in 1881. At that time, the shop was owned by Henry Luerssen, for whom Schering worked as a wagon maker. They also sold machinery.

This is the same scene on Slade Street in the 1940s. A corner of the Palatine Hospital Building can be seen on the right. Super Service Stores is next to it. On the corner is the State Bank of Palatine, which later housed a beauty school. The street ends at Railroad Avenue. The railroad crossing at Plum Grove Road can be seen in the distance.

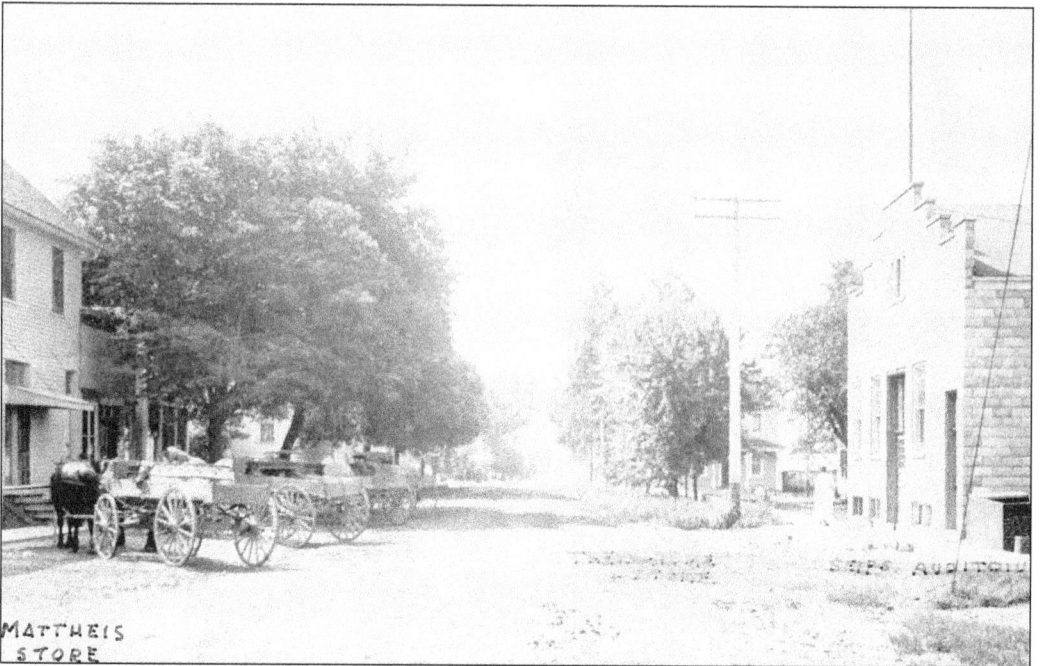

Looking south on Bothwell from Slade Street, *c.* 1910, Matthei's Store is on the left (east) corner. The Seip Auditorium (or Hall), on the right, was built in 1908 adjoining Seip's Hotel and Tavern on Slade Street (later Annex Hotel). Charlie Siep and his wife, Minnie Fink, operated the hotel her father had purchased in 1870. The Seip Hall later became the Palatine (movie) Theater and once showed the film *Right Foot Forward*, which was made in Palatine.

Matthei's Store stood on the corner of Bothwell and Slade Streets, *c.* 1920. Down Railroad Avenue, the building at the left across Plum Grove Road is the Masonic Hall of Palatine Lodge No. 314, built in 1905. It is still serving the same purpose. There was once a bowling alley on the lower floor. Church and Sunday school sessions have been held there. For a time, the Palatine Library was located there.

Looking down Bothwell Street from Slade Street, c. the late 1930s, Matthei's building is on the east, and the State Bank of Palatine is on the west. Seip's Hall, behind the bank, now sports a marquee since it has become a movie house. The first Palatine Library can be seen behind Matthei's. Matthei's would be torn down and replaced with the Pepper Block Building, which extended down Bothwell almost to Palatine Road.

August Kimmet and his wife, Caroline Katherine Teufert, came to Palatine in 1876. Mrs. Kimmet operated a millinery shop in this building on the northwest corner of Slade and Greeley Streets for 36 years. August Kimmet was the last living Civil War veteran residing in Palatine.

This W.E. Schering Blacksmith Shop is believed to have been in the building on Slade Street where Luerssen's had operated. Standing in front of the building, from left to right, are Louis Nerge, Elmer Peterson, August Kimmet, Chris Schering, and William Schering. William Schering was the oldest active blacksmith in Illinois when he retired in 1953 at age 85.

Louis Nerge and William Schering are working inside Schering's Shoeing Shop. Other wisdom has it that Schering's was located on the south side of Wood Street, west of Brockway Street, instead of in the Luerssen's Building. It is possible he began at Luerssen's and moved to a second site.

Bowman Dairy built this milk plant in 1906 at Wood and Smith Streets. At the time, it was the largest and most complete bottling plant along the Chicago and Northwestern Railroad line. Bowman had six plants in the area from which they shipped 14 rail cars of bottled milk and cream to Chicago daily.

Inside the Bowman Dairy, this bottling machine traveled on a track above a metallic table. An operator turned a crank that tilted the machine. Rubber discs fit snugly into the mouths of the bottles, automatically receding when they were filled. The plant used 25 tons of ice per day to pack the cases of milk for delivery.

CLARENCE
COLLIGNON

CHICAGO + ROSE
1931

HENRY
COLLIGNON

The Palatine Dairy was operated by Albert L. Collignon and Sons (Clarence, Raymond, Albert, Henry, and Vernon). They were located at 302 West Chicago Avenue (Palatine Road), at the corner of Rose Street. They continued in business until the 1940s.

The Gaare Family lived and owned land at Colfax and Smith Streets, south of Hillside Cemetery. When Northwest Highway was routed through Palatine in the 1920s down Colfax Street, the family built this service station and facility. This is an August 1936, photograph of their Daisy Service Station.

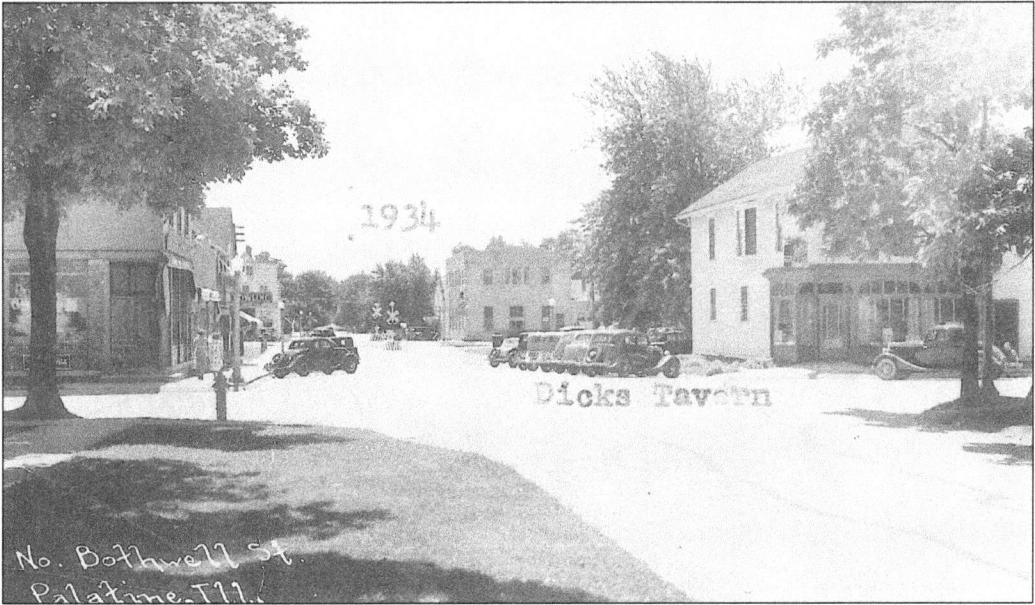

This 1934 photograph is looking down Bothwell Street from Wilson, toward the tracks. The building marked Dick's (Sanford) Tavern had been built in 1860 as the first Masonic Hall. It had housed a meeting hall, barber shop, bakery, and other shops and had been used as a schoolroom during the Civil War. It is now the Lamplighter Inn.

Dick Sanford is waiting on customers in his tavern on North Bothwell in 1936. One morning, a Palatine resident came into the tavern and shot Sanford's daughter Alice and piano player Ed Batterman. The killer then shot himself. Both the gunman and Batterman died that night. Alice spent the rest of her life in a nursing home with a bullet lodged in her head.

This building, housing Rennack's Market, was located on the southeast corner of Bothwell and Wilson Streets, across from Dick's Tavern in this 1934 photograph. The Carl Rennack family had come to Palatine in 1893. His son Charles operated this meat market. Charles's son Walter was president of the Palatine Library Board for many years, and the large meeting room in the Benton Street facility was named for him.

Although Fred Folleth had learned the shoemaker's trade before he came to Palatine in 1881, he spent most of his life farming. When Cook County Forest Preserve District took 20 acres of his farm for Deer Grove, he sold the farm and moved to Palatine. In 1920, he opened this shoe store at 57 North Bothwell Street and operated it for seven years. It is now Dirty Nellie's Pub.

Five

PRIVATE LIVES

Mr. and Mrs. Henry C. Batterman stand in front of their house on the corner of Greeley and Johnson Streets. The house was built in 1902, and the Battermans lived in it until 1905. Batterman owned the land from here north to Palatine Road, which had been the site of his flax mill, built in 1878, and the planing mill, built in 1882. Both burned down in 1892. Batterman came to Palatine in 1866 and was in the grain and lumber business with John Slade. He later consolidated with Abelman and Ost, owners of an elevator. In 1884, he erected the Batterman Brick Block Building. As president of the Palatine Board of Trustees from 1896 to 1898, he could often be seen with a shovel and pickax doing small repairs on the business streets. Batterman retired in 1925. The site of this house is now a small shopping center.

Dr. William P. Schirding built this home at the corner of Wilson and Brockway Streets in the 1890s. Schirding was an ear, nose, and throat specialist and had an office in this house and another in Chicago. By 1929, this was an empty lot and remained so for many years. Eventually, a new building housed the Jewel Food Store, S&H Green Stamp Redemption store, a Ben Franklin, and now Mia Cucina Restaurant.

Rollin S. Williamson built this house (shown in 1909). He came to Palatine in 1887 and was a state representative, a senator, and a judge in superior court. After his death, his widow, Emma, married Dr. Elias E. Wood in 1895. She continued to live in the house until her death in 1921 but spent her winters in California. The site is now part of Immanuel Lutheran Church School parking lot.

This is the east side of Bothwell Street, north of Wilson. The Swick house is nearest, then the Sutherland home. Nancy Boynton came to Palatine Township in 1838 with her parents and married Mason Sutherland, who had arrived with his family in 1837. Boynton's parents owned a farm at Dundee and Hicks Roads. In the 1850s, the Boynton family built this brick house at the corner of Bothwell and Wood Streets.

Standing in front of the Sutherland house, c. 1888, are Nancy Sutherland, daughter Emma Sutherland Matthei, and granddaughter Annie Matthei Brockway. Annie's daughter, Mae Brockway Howes, had a daughter, Georgiana Howes Palmer, who still lives in Palatine. Nancy's husband, Mason, died during service in the Civil War, after which her family continued to live on income from their farm.

Lottie Emma Hart came with her family to this house at Oak Street and Chicago Avenue (Palatine Road) in the 1880s. She lived here until her death in 1953. Lottie Hart was the first librarian of Palatine in 1923 and served in that capacity until 1950. This site is now a parking lot.

This house at Benton Street and Palatine Road was built in 1892 by Albert L. Smith to replace his brick house, which burned down the year before. The house has been beautifully restored by its present owners and was featured in the 1997 Palatine Historical Society House Walk. Cemetery Road, north of the tracks, was renamed Smith Street because the family owned a farm there.

Mrs. Michael Sneible and her sons, George and Walter, stand in front of their *c.* 1870 house, which is still standing at the corner of Colfax and Hale Streets. Michael Snieble's father, John, had come from Rome, New York, to a farm near Palatine in 1868. In 1883, he moved into town and worked as a carpenter. Michael was a janitor at the Joel Wood School.

This is the garden behind the Sneible house, a typical scene about 1900. The Sneible boys remained in Palatine. Walter followed his father as custodian of the Joel Wood School for 41 years, while George worked at the drug store when Zinn owned it.

Charles H. Patten, a Palatine banker and mayor from 1894 to 1895, had this house designed by a French architect and built in 1898. Today, it is central Palatine's largest and most distinctive home. It is on a large lot within two blocks of the village hall, Sanborn School, and Clayson House. A member of the Patten family still lives in the house.

William Ost built this home about 1920 after Herman Stroker removed an earlier house. Ost was a member of the high school board of education. The field behind the 1928 high school building was named for him. In 1958, the house was sold to the Palatine Library for $25,000. When the library moved in 1975, the building (with its addition) became the Unitarian Church and is now a Korean Church.

The George Schweitzer house stood at Chicago Avenue (Palatine Road) and Rose Street. The smallest child is identified as his daughter Dora and the bigger girl is Emma, daughter of Schweitzer's first wife, Louise Krieter. "X" marks "Old Grandpa Diekman," who was the father of George's second wife, Augusta. This photo is probably from the 1880s. George Schweitzer, a contract builder, died in 1889. His wife, Augusta, went to work as a housekeeper for the Wesley Comfort family. The Schweitzers had 12 children, 10 of whom died before Augusta's death in 1925.

Charles and Caroline Ost stand in front of their house at the southeast corner of Greeley and Chicago Avenue (Palatine Road). This house stood across the street from the family's grain and lumber mill, which burned down. Ost was in business with Batterman and Abelman. His various enterprises included a flour mill, a planing and grinding mill, and lumber and coal businesses. He retired in 1906. Ost was on the board of trustees in 1897 when he helped push through plans for the water works. He served as a board member again from 1904 to 1916. For many years, Heng Wing Chinese Restaurant has occupied this site.

Albert S. and Augusta Olms moved to this house at 52 West Colfax in 1888. Olms, a pharmacist, purchased the F.B. Robinson Drug Store on the west side of Brockway, which would later be known as Coleman's. The house is still standing but has been altered and is now a chiropractor's office.

David Lytle, born in 1821 in the East, came to Palatine with his parents, William and Rebecca. He lived in this house at 54 North Plum Grove Road. The house has had many residents in the years since, including the Johnson, Alverson, Rennack, Pahlman, Porter, Dr. Ross, Mair, Wienecke, Seip, and Crabtree families.

The brick house on the northeast corner of Colfax Street and Plum Grove Road was built in 1870 of Kitson brick. Two porches were later added, one of which can be seen in this 1923 photograph. John Kitson had learned the pottery trade in England, so when he came to Palatine, he operated a brickyard behind the family home on Quentin Road north of Palatine Road.

This house, at the southeast corner of Brockway and Wood Streets, was built in 1905 by Henrietta Matthei Schirding. For a time, the house served as St. Theresa Convent and later was occupied by the Martin Plates. Plate served 11 years on the Village of Palatine Board of Trustees and 14 years on the Palatine High School Board. Rita Mullins, president of the board of trustees, now lives in the house.

On April 6, 1930, Palatine Catholics celebrated their first Mass on the second floor of the old village hall at 117 West Slade Street. They rented the facility following the construction of the new municipal building on Brockway Street that year. Note the cross on the roof. St. Theresa Catholic Church remained in this facility until they dedicated their first church building on Wood and Bothwell Streets in 1941.

With the rapid growth in Palatine after WW II, St. Theresa quickly outgrew this building on Wood Street. A school was built on North Benton in 1954 and expanded twice. A new church and convent were added at the site in 1960 and an activities center in 1979. The 1941 building in this photo became Santa Teresita Church and was renamed Mision Juan Diego in 1999. It is the only Spanish church in the Chicago Archdiocese where only Spanish is spoken, according to Rev. Moises Marin, the church director.

Through the years, Immanuel Lutheran Church has been located on the block between Wood and Colfax Streets and Plum Grove and Bothwell Streets. The first wooden church was purchased from the Disciple Church in 1870 and used until 1914. The imposing church structure in this photo was erected in 1914 and served until a new, larger modern facility was built in 1970.

This two-story brick Immanuel Lutheran School was built in 1926 on the site of an older building that was sold and moved. There have been additions to the school, including a gymnasium. Classes are held for preschool through eighth grade. Today, the church and school building occupy the greater part of a city block.

Pastor Daniel Poellet served the Immanuel Lutheran Church from 1910 to 1940. In this photo, he stands in front of the parsonage at 14 West Wood Street with his sons Daniel, Luther, and Herbert; his wife, Lillie; and her mother, Lusette Breuggemann. All three of the Poellet sons became ministers.

St. Paul's United Church of Christ began in 1870, when Pastor Krueger of St. John's Church in Plum Grove began holding services in the old Masonic Hall on North Bothwell. This wooden church building, erected on Chicago Avenue (Palatine Road), and a school, built in 1888, served the congregation until 1925.

81

This brick building of St. Paul's United Church of Christ at 144 East Palatine Road was dedicated in 1925, and an educational addition was completed in 1955. The Palatine Historical Society has been able to duplicate records from the church, many of which had to be translated from German.

In this May 1885, confirmation class picture of St. Paul's United Church of Christ are, from left to right, as follows: (front row) Herman Berlin, Bertha Bicknase, Mary Boeck, Sophie Gusewelle, and Henry Wildehagen; (back row) Reverend Geibel, Minnie Mavis, Louise Tegtmeier, Minnie Fink Seip, Clara Meier, and Emma Kublank Westrope.

The Salem Evangelical Church was built in the early 1890s, north of Kirchoff Road on Plum Grove Road. The site had held a much earlier building that was struck by lightening. In 1912, the church building was moved into town on Plum Grove Road at Lincoln Street. The congregation disbanded in 1955, and the building was sold to Immanuel Lutheran Church.

This Salem Evangelical Church Cemetery adjoined the church, which no longer exists, on Plum Grove Road, north of Kirchoff Road. This little corner of quiet now sits at a busy intersection. Behind it, a strip mall and parking lot have been built. Long ago, there were also tombstones on the south side of Kirchoff Road, but these no longer exist.

The 1895 First United Methodist Church was designed by Rev. William Smith and built by Joseph Wenegar on the site of an earlier church. The land on Plum Grove Road at Wood Street was donated by Joel Wood. A new sanctuary in 1958 and an education wing in 1969 have been added. Restoration of this building was completed in 1976, with the work being done almost entirely by members of the congregation.

Six

PEOPLE

Members of the 1907 graduating class of Palatine High School are, from left to right, Marion Taylor, Cora Bergman, Grace Van Horne, John Godknecht, and Cassandra (Cassie) Gainer. Marion Taylor's father, Clifford De Witt Taylor, served as mayor of Palatine from 1914 to 1920. Cora Bergman's family came to America in 1853. Her grandfather, Louis Bergmann, served in the Civil War. Cora was born in Palatine and taught school for nine years. She died at age 28. Grace Van Horne came to Palatine with her family in 1853. She married Marvin Greener, and they lived at 104 North Plum Grove Road (The house is no longer there.). John Godknecht grew up in the house at 137 North Plum Grove Road where his father Henry manufactured cigars. A wooden cigar store Indian (now belonging to the Palatine Historical Society) stood on the porch. The 1872 house is still standing. Cassandra Gainer's grandparents were early settlers in the area. Cassandra died in 1973.

The Prellberg family, standing in front of their home and shop at 19 West Railroad Avenue, are, from left to right, as follows: Henry, William, Charles, George, Minnie, Sophie, mother Sophie, and father Ernest. The Prellbergs had 15 children, some of whom died very young. Ernest married Sophie Heideman in 1873 after the death of his first wife, Johanna.

This is a formal portrait of the Ernest Prellberg family. Ernest had established his "Merchant Tailor" business in 1865. In 1900, he was contracted by the Palatine Volunteer Fire Department to make 18 blue suits. Sons William and Charles took over the business after their father's death in 1922. The tailor shop building was torn down in 1975, at which time it was the oldest business building still standing in Palatine.

The Kuebler family are, from left to right, (front row) Rose, Harry, and father Isaac; (back row) Emeline, mother Lena, and George. The Kueblers came to Palatine in the 1870s and occupied a house at Bothwell and Colfax Streets, which has been restored by the present owners. Lena's parents operated the Kuebler-Hunnerberg Hotel, next to the tracks. The hall adjoining the hotel was used for dances and parties. The Palatine High School basketball team practiced there.

The Ost family are, from left to right, Caroline, Edward, Charles, William, and Charles W. The family lived on their farm in Ela Township and moved to Palatine in 1887. Charles was in business with Abelman and Ost in their mills. He sold the flour mill to his son William in 1903. Charles served as chief of Palatine's Volunteer Fire Department from 1907 to 1917. William became chief in 1917, serving until 1933.

The Battermans and Abelmans were related by marriage as well as in business. In this c. 1908 photo are the following, from left to right: (front row) Lillian Abelman, Delia Batterman Krueger, and Edward Batterman; (seated) August Abelman; (standing) Bertha Batterman, Louise Batterman Abelman, and Marie Berger (a seamstress from Chicago).

This was a fine day in the early 1900s to be swinging in the back yard for these people. They are, from left to right, Margaret Godknecht, Delia Knigge, Harry Bergman (or possibly Bill Mundhenk), Betsy Torgler Thompson, and Hattie Kuebler. Margaret Godknecht lived at 137 North Plum Grove Road, the house of her father, the cigar maker. Betsy Torgler Thompson's mother, Henrietta, was Palatine's first switchboard operator in 1902.

This is a very early class sitting on the steps of the 1868 wooden Joel Wood School Building. To date, no one has been able to identify the children or teacher in this photograph.

These people are believed to be Palatine High School students, identified as graduating between 1895 and 1904. There are a number of siblings and/or cousins in this photo. For example, there are two Mundhenks, four Bicknases, two Abelmans, two Wieneckes, three Kueblers, and a Godknecht, Mosser, Danielson, Horstman, Knigge, and Bergman. The high school operated on the top floor of the old wooden Joel Wood School.

Charles Sidney Cutting was 20 years old when he came to Palatine to teach at the Joel Wood School in 1874. The following year, he became principal and started Palatine High School, a two-year course and the only high school between Jefferson Park and Woodstock. In 1876, Cutting married Annie Lytle, whose father, Myron, had opened a grocery in 1856, only six years after Palatine Township was founded. Myron had also served as the first mayor after the Village of Palatine was incorporated in 1866. Charles Cutting continued his studies and was admitted to the bar in 1880. He went into law practice with Rollin Williamson of Palatine, and, from 1899 to 1913, he was a judge of the probate court. Though he moved to Austin (now Chicago) in 1895, he never lost touch with Palatine High School. He gave many gifts to the school library. The auditorium, which was named in his honor, is the only remaining portion of the 1928 high school building, and it is still known as Cutting Hall.

Charles F. Rennack and Emma Caroline Pahlman were married on March 27, 1895. Charles owned a meat market at 61 North Bothwell Street, which he opened on Oct. 12, 1906. Emma's grandparents had settled on a farm north of Palatine in 1853 and moved to town in 1865. Her parents, Herman and Annie, lived in the house at 60 East Slade Street, which still stands.

This is a picture of the Pahlman brothers and sisters. Their mother, Mary Rantzen Pahlman, is the small woman in the center. She died in 1906. Her brother Herman, in the center, was the father of Emma, who married Charles Rennack in 1895.

Caroline Teufert and August Kimmet were married June 16, 1871. At age 17, August enlisted in the Civil War. He was wounded and captured by the Confederates and, while still in the hospital, was rescued by the Union Army. He was a carpenter and general handyman, and Caroline Kimmet operated a millinery store for 36 years. The Kimmets built the house at the northwest corner of Smith and Slade Streets in 1872.

This wedding photo is of Orville Helms's grandparents, Fred and Wilhelmina Helms. Orville spent 42 years with the Palatine Fire Department, 23 of those years as chief. He was the first chief of the all-professional department. He also served on the police force and was a school district trustee. Orville Helms has been a valuable resource for the Palatine Historical Society.

Alma Othmer was born in 1894, the daughter of two early Palatine Township residents, Minnie Tegtmeier and Henry Othmer. Her parents moved into Palatine at 223 West Wilson Street in about 1902. This is a wedding photo of Alma Othmer and Henry Heitman. The couple resided in Palatine.

This is the July 6, 1935, marriage of Vera Pohlman to Charles Klopp. On the left is Vera's sister Bea (Wenegar), and on the right is her sister Lysette (Donkin). Charles Klopp was an architect and chairman of the Palatine Plan Commission. The Pohlman family lived on a farm on Rand Road before moving into town in 1927.

Augusta "Gussie" Olms was nine years old in this 1887 photo. She was born in Gilman, Illinois, before her family moved to Palatine in 1888. Gussie was an assistant cashier at the Palatine State Bank. In 1929, Gussie resided with her parents at 52 North Colfax Street. She later lived in St. Petersburg, Florida, with her brother Frank.

This photograph of Albert S. Olms was taken about the same time as that of his daughter Gussie, above. Olms was a pharmacist, and he purchased C. Robinson Drug when he first came to Palatine. Later, he dealt in real estate and served as village president in 1893 and again from 1899 to 1908.

These people, who are posing in the Palatine Community Hospital, have not been identified. Dr. Carl A. Starck established the hospital in 1916 because he wanted a "more proper place than the farm home" in which to deliver babies. The hospital quickly expanded as the demand for beds rose. Nurses were trained in the facility, which operated until 1950.

Mrs. Burlingame; Bill Peck; his mother, Mrs. Ralph (Caroline) Peck; and Mrs. Floyd (Rose Wilson) Gibbs pose in this photo. The Pecks lived at 328 North Plum Grove Road. Ralph Peck served as village attorney and was president of the school board. As president of the Palatine National Bank, he was indicted on charges of embezzling $25,000 for which he was sentenced to 18 months in prison and fined $2,500.

Clarence Comfort and Wesley Comfort Jr. continued W.R. Comfort and Sons after the death of their father in 1926. The company had begun in 1874 operating a grain elevator under the name of Comfort and Slade (W.R.'s father-in-law). In 1968, the Comfort building and lumber yard was razed, and the Palatine National Bank (now Harris Bank) occupied their new building on the site. Wesley was a volunteer fireman for 30 years and fire chief for 15 years. His son, Wesley III, also a volunteer fireman, was killed in 1946 when the fire truck on which he was riding collided with a train at the Brockway Street crossing. Clarence retired from the family business in 1958 and died in 1960. The Palatine Historical Society has been the recipient of a great deal of archival material from the Comfort family business.

This happy group is celebrating the wedding anniversary of Irene and Paul Wilson, who stand in the back row, third and fourth from left. The "bride" is Gilbert Fosket, whose family has a street named after them. The "bridesmaid" is Harry Kincaid, a Palatine High School coach in the 1920s. The "groom" is Isabelle Stroker, and the "groomsman" is Mildred Sanborn. Mildred's husband, Gray, behind her, has a school named after him.

This photo is of the 1886 class of the Joel Wood School. The teacher is Persis Hicks. Many family names are duplicated among these students, since the population of Palatine was small. Often families arrived with several siblings, who in turn had numerous children. Many of the families were interrelated by marriage or marriages.

Elmer and Esther Wenegar, shown here in a *c.* 1912 photo, were two of four children born to Benjamin and Bertha Wenegar. Benjamin had followed his father's footsteps as a builder, the brick Joel Wood School being one of his projects. Grandpa Jacob Wenegar built the first village hall and the Plum Grove and Methodist Churches. Elmer was married to Beatrice Pohlman.

ELMER WENEGAR (THE
ESTHER WENEGAR SCH

William "Billy" Mair Jr., in the center, is celebrating his birthday, *c.* 1929. His father, William, was a supervisor of country plants for Bowman Dairy. His mother taught third grade at the Joel Wood School for many years. Billy never married and died at age 39 in 1943.

Seven

LEISURE ACTIVITIES

Players on this Palatine football team are as follows, from left to right: (front row) Lee Bissell, Philip Matthei, H.L. Merrill (or W.L. Smyser), and Walter Lytle; (back row) William Mosser, A.G. Smith, Bert L. Smith, Henry Pohlman, Earl Dahms, Harry Rea, and J. Fink. This photo is dated 1894. Since the uniforms are emblazoned with PHS, it was assumed to be the Palatine High School football team. However, the son of A.G. Smith said his father never attended Palatine High, and the school did not have a football team then. He identifies the team as the Palatine Men's Athletic Club, *c.* 1900. Whatever explanation is accurate, the picture is a treasure for the football itself. Have you ever seen one that shape?

A Cook County Fair was held annually in Palatine from 1914 until about 1929. This is a 1923 photograph of the entrance to the fair, which was located east of present-day Northwest Highway and Hicks Road, roughly in the area of the K-Mart Mall on the north and Palanois Park Subdivision on the south. The fair contained all of the elements one would expect at a fair: displays, judging, entertainment, animals, and food.

Charles Dean operated harness racing at his track, which was the site of the Cook County Fair. He also boarded and trained animals for Chicago horsemen in the early years of the century. His stables and half-mile track drew many visitors. In the above picture, the horses are lined up at the judges' stand. There was a grandstand for viewing the races as well as entertainment between races.

Deer Grove Park was operated by Dr. J.W. Wilson in the forest at Dundee and Quentin Roads. On weekends, people came to Palatine by train (and later by car) to enjoy the outdoors as well as the dance pavilion, running track, baseball field, refreshment parlor, and dining hall. In 1915, Cook County purchased Deer Grove as the first property in its Forest Preserve District.

When it was still a private park, families would come out to stay in these primitive quarters for a vacation. There were some permanent houses where people continued to live after the property was sold. The Forest Preserve District offered everyone the opportunity to move the houses out of the park. Some moved to the Gainer Park and Teonia Woods subdivisions.

This group, inside the Kunze Saloon (southeast corner of Brockway and Slade Streets) in the early 1900s, seem to be having a grand time. They are, from left to right, as follows: (seated) William Henning, Fred Henning, Henry Hitzeman, and Charles Streus; (standing) Charles Henning, Henry Bruhns, Fred ?, Grandpa Meyer, Henry Roesner Sr., Al Smith, Fred Gieske, and August Hackbarth.

This aerial photo of the Arlington Park Race Track, with the Wilke farm across Northwest Highway, was taken about 1955. The track was built in 1927 by H.D. "Curley" Brown from California. His investors survived the Depression by attracting top horses and jockeys and with innovations such as the first electric exact-odds tote board and high-speed motion picture camera for close finishes. Ben Lindheimer and his associates bought the track in 1940, and his daughter Marjorie Everett ran it after his death in 1960 until 1971. Richard Duchossois became sole owner in 1986. On July 31, 1985, the grandstand, shown here, burned down. The Arlington Million was run at the track only 25 days after the fire. Debris had been cleared, a temporary bleacher erected, and 43 tents set up. A beautiful new Arlington Park International Race Track was rebuilt in 1989.

This July Fourth parade took place in 1917 during World War I. The procession is passing the bandstand, and the Schoppe Brothers' float had just passed by. Palatine continues to hold July Fourth parades plus several days of carnivals, arts and crafts, and food booths, sponsored for many years by the Palatine Jaycees. The Palatine Historical Society produces a float every year

This bandstand stood at the northwest corner of Brockway and Slade Streets until it was removed in 1921, when the Palatine National Bank was built. The Palatine Military Band gave summer concerts each week in this bandstand.

Here was an early form of entertainment around 1910. These dancing bears are in front of Matthei's Store at Slade and Bothwell Streets. The man in back with the bald head is Philip Matthei, and the girl in the plaid dress is Mae Brockway (Howes) with Helen Matthei to her right. George Matthei is the man in black.

It is November 1913, and a vaudeville show will be in town Saturday night. We're at Bothwell and Wilson Streets with Rennack's Meat Market (a Mexican restaurant now) in the left background. Frye's Livery Barn (now Dirty Nellie's Pub) is on the end, and Jacob Burhardt's Shoe Repair is sandwiched in the middle.

The Palatine Maennerchor, pictured here in 1890, was a German men's singing society, which existed for about 40 years. It cherished the songs of Germany and fostered the feeling of good fellowship and intellectual enjoyment among its members. In December 1917, the group disbanded because only a few members of the old guard remained. It was a community power and a leader in society and in social events because many of its members were representatives of the leading German-American families of Palatine.

One form of entertainment in small towns was a locally produced and acted play. Over the years, many of them were presented by the churches. This play (or perhaps a pageant) was a production of the First United Methodist Church about 1930.

St. Paul United Church of Christ produced this program with these sporty-looking ladies in the early 1900s. The participants are Alma Bicknase, Mary Hoffmeister (the minister's daughter), Lillian Abelman (Hake), Margaret Godknecht, Hatti Kuebler, Delia Knigge (Flaherty), and Emma Godknecht.

Sidney Page, a Palatine resident and president of the Lions Club in 1939–1940, was active in vaudeville for 40 years. He founded the Sidney J. Page Theatrical Agency in Chicago. His wife, Peggy, and her sister, Kathryn, were dancers. In this photo (probably from the 1920s), they are posed for one for their performances.

The Palatine Lions Club was organized in 1925 at a time of unrest in the town. It had a charter membership of 25 prominent local men and had the aim of bringing unity and worthwhile projects to Palatine.

108

This photo of Boy Scout Troop 9 can be dated about 1921 because of the presence of Rev. S.E. Pollack (rear center), who served the Methodist Church in 1921–22. At various times, George Miniberger, Harry Kincaid, and John Manz acted as scoutmasters. In 1946, the Palatine Lions Club sponsored Troop 9, which was reorganized under Scoutmaster Ray Mills. There are many scout troops in Palatine today, but there is no Troop 9.

The Palatine Military Band was organized by J.H. Schierding in the 1870s and continued to operate until 1935. The band always led the Memorial Day Parade and gave weekly concerts in the bandstand until 1921. Early on the Fourth of July morning, the band toured the town on a haywagon, playing stirring music. This photo was probably taken around the turn of the century.

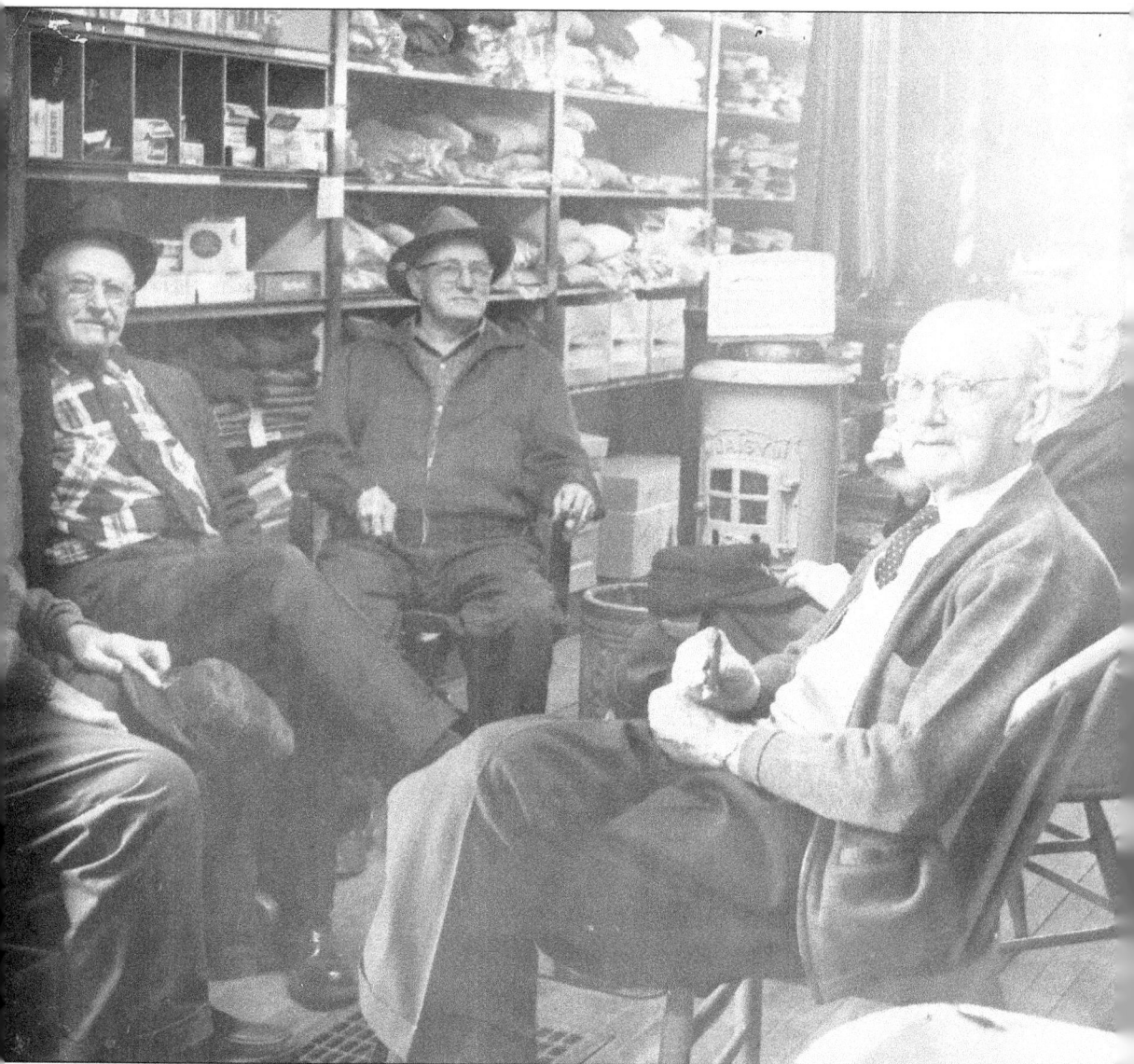

Schoppe's General Store was such an institution in Palatine that when the store celebrated its 70th anniversary in 1964, Village President Wilbur D. Harris declared April 1–7, 1964, as "Harry Schoppe Week." Old-timers used to gather around the pot-bellied stove in the store for warm conversation and storytelling. When the building burned down in 1970, both Fire Chief Orville Helms and Police Chief Robert Centner recalled "old man Schoppe" giving them candy when they were kids. In this photo are, from left to right, Max Lines, Henry Kincaid, Charles Thorp, and Harry Schoppe. The Schoppe Store closed in 1967. A look at Schoppe's December 1894, hand-written ledger of sales is fascinating: coffee, 25 ¢; sugar, 25 ¢; oil, 10 ¢; eight-pound turkey, 80 ¢; toys, 42 ¢; shoes, $1.75; cup and saucer, 21 ¢; dolls, 30 ¢; baby carriage, 50 ¢; apron goods, 21 ¢; and dress goods, 30 ¢.

This building, now at the busy corner of Palatine and Plum Grove Roads, looked like this when it was built as a Masonic Hall in 1905 by Palatine Lodge No. 314 Ancient, Free, and Accepted Masons. The facility was also used as a dining room and hall for community meetings. Immanuel Lutheran Church held their first services there. The building is still the Chapter 314 Masonic Hall.

The Modern Woodman of America was a fraternal organization, which is now largely an insurance company. It was an active organization with initiation stunts that rivaled those of college fraternities. Palatine Camp No. 6395 is pictured here with their equipment. A drill team was part of the organization.

Palatine Rebekkah Lodge #116 Auxiliary of the Independent Order of Odd Fellows was organized in 1925. In this presentation are, from left to right, as follows: (front row) Alvina Mess, Mary Lewis, Clara Wienecke, Augusta Ohms as bride, Florence Parkhurst as groom, Emma Vogt, Emeline Godknecht, and Catherine Moose; (back row) Gertrude Smith, Lena Deverman, Anna Holdeman, and Laura Wagner.

This must have been the Palatine Garden Club's first show, held in the lobby of the new State Bank of Palatine building on opening day, June 6, 1931. The group had been organized in March of that year. Mae Howes, Mayme Mangels, Cora Comfort, Elnora Foster, Lillian Bergman, and Lottie Hart display their efforts. For many years, a major project of the group was the maintenance of the depot park.

Someone made ingenious use of this privately owned empty lot by putting up a net. The tennis game is being played on dirt. It makes you wonder how the ball bounced. The lot, located on the east side of Hale, halfway between Colfax and Lincoln Streets, now holds a house.

This was one way to enjoy the winter. These people are taking advantage of a nice day after a snowstorm in 1908. It looks like someone just got hit with a snowball. Of course, the child on the sled is having a great ride.

The Palatine Athletic Club is shown playing football on February 22, 1918. They are posed here at Washington and Smith Streets. Only F. Hunneberg and George Voss have been identified in this group.

This Palatine basketball team in 1940 was sponsored by Dinse's Bowling, Pool, Billiards and Barber Shop Emporium. The team was known as "Dinse's Recs." They played a regular season of 12 or 15 games against teams stretching from Zion to Elgin. Another team at this time was sponsored by Adolf Kunze's Pure Oil Gas Station (Plum Grove and Palatine Roads) called "Kunze's Oilers." Teams were well supported by the townspeople.

In April 1914, the Palatine High School baseball team sits on the steps of the new Joel Wood School. They are, from left to right, as follows: (front row) Treasurer Arthur Wienecke, Robert Brodhay, Leslie Freye, Captain George Herrman, and Lawrence Freye; (middle row) Martin Goetz, Ira Cook, Robert Fosket, Manager John F. Gainer, Secretary Olin Umdenstock, and Adolph Kunze; (back row) Irving Behling, Gordon Humphrey, Assistant Manager Paul Pohlman, and Principal C. A. Wells.

Harrison Kincaid was coach of the 1930–31 Palatine High School basketball team, which was the champion of the Northwest Conference. Kincaid was coaching a Palatine High team even before the school acquired a gymnasium in 1928. The players are, from left to right, Wilbert Cole, Harris Helgeson, Orville Helms, and Harold Meyer, with Elmer Mess seated in front.

The government may have legislated equal opportunity sports in recent years, but Palatine High School was ahead of the game, as seen in this 1916–1917 girls' basketball team. The school did not have a gymnasium at the time because they were located in the brick Joel Wood School. Practice was probably held at Hunnerberg Hall. Team members are as follows, from left to right: (front row) Mildred Smith and Dorothy Timmerman; (middle row) Ruth Schering, Myra Smith, Lulu Simmons, Edna Timmerman, and Jennie Hanns; (back row) Madge Gibbs, Helen Matthei, Helen Swick, Coach Heinz, Dorothy Gibbs, Grace Vogt, and Frances Daniels

Eight

WARS AND
OTHER DISASTERS

Fifty surviving Civil War veterans of the 113th Illinois Volunteer Infantry held one of their reunions in Palatine on September 14, 1910. Company E was recruited from Palatine and the surrounding area. A window in the 1895 Methodist Church commemorates the organization of the unit on August 11, 1862. The regiment was mustered into service in October 1862, and returned to Chicago in June 1865. The regiment participated in the principal battles fought for the possession of Vicksburg. The Palatine men in this 1910 group are Fred Timmerman, Charles Fosket, Charles Robinson, A.R. Baldwin, John Hamilton , Dr. Osbourn, Bert Webster, M. Umdenstock, H. Swick, and A. Maloney. Exact identification is unknown. Nancy Boynton Sutherland, widow of Capt. Mason Sutherland, was present, though in feeble health, and was carried to the gathering in a chair.

Company E of the 113th Illinois Volunteers was known as the "Bradwell Guard" because Judge James B. Bradwell, shown here, was active in its organization. The Bradwell family came to the area in 1834. Mason Sutherland received permission from Governor Yates to form Company E, and he was appointed captain. The regiment gathered at Camp Hancock in Chicago and left for Tennessee and Mississippi the 6th of November in 1862.

Mason Sutherland's family came to Palatine in 1837, and Mason married Nancy Boynton in 1843. A few hours before his company was to leave for the south, Mason rushed home to help with the harvest. It was the last time his family saw him. He contracted typhoid fever and died January 27, 1863, in Young's Point, Louisiana.

Louis Bergmann was the son of Jean Louis and Margaret Bergmann, who had came to Palatine from the German colony of Alsace-Lorraine in 1855 and eventually lived on a farm on Algonquin Road, west of Roselle Road. Louis fought in the 113th Illinois Infantry and was captured in Mississippi at the Battle of Brices Cross Roads. He died in a prisoner of war camp in Georgia.

This memorial and cannon sat in Railroad Park, located north of the original station. It appears to be the one now in Hillside Cemetery. The metal plate is gone, and the stone has these words engraved on it: "To those who sleep in unknown graves." Sitting next to it is the barrel of a cannon, thought to be the one in this photo. The wooden base and wheels probably rotted.

This is a photo taken to publicize the sale of WW I Liberty Bonds in the 4th Liberty Loan Drive. In a letter from H.H. Pahlman, chairman for District No. 102, War Loan Organization, residents were urged to subscribe $100. The bonds were being offered on April 20th, probably in 1919, as Pahlman refers to them as "Victory" Liberty Bonds which "enable us to pay for Victory with money instead of the lives of our American boys." The subscription drive in Palatine was on Saturday and Sunday, April 19th and 20th, at Palatine Headquarters, Hackbarth's Garage, the building where these men are standing. Besides "Tires" and "Case" (farm equipment) advertised on the windows, August Hackbarth sold new cars. In 1915, he had advertised a Maxwell 25 for $655, including electric starter and electric lights. Hey, remember Jack Benny's Maxwell! The building has been occupied by Marmax Glass and Mirror since 1972.

The WW I soldier in this photo is Lt. J.L. Rawson, husband of Thelma Olms. The family is celebrating the golden wedding anniversary of Albert and Augusta Olms. They are as follows, from left to right: (front row) Lt. J. L. and Thelma Rawson and Albert Rush Putnam; (middle row) Edna's mother, Albert and Augusta Olms; (back row) Edna and Frank Olms, Dr. Rush and Minnie Putnam, and Gussie Olms.

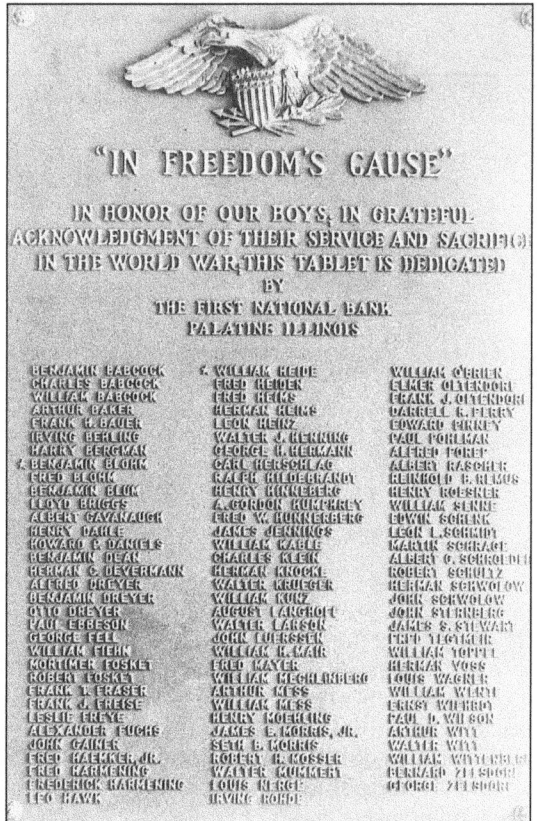

"IN FREEDOM'S CAUSE"

IN HONOR OF OUR BOYS, IN GRATEFUL ACKNOWLEDGMENT OF THEIR SERVICE AND SACRIFICE IN THE WORLD WAR, THIS TABLET IS DEDICATED BY THE FIRST NATIONAL BANK PALATINE ILLINOIS

BENJAMIN BABCOCK	C. WILLIAM HEIDE	WILLIAM O'BRIEN
CHARLES BABCOCK	FRED HEIDEN	ELMER OLTENDORF
WILLIAM BABCOCK	FRED HEIMS	FRANK J. OLTENDORF
ARTHUR BAKER	HERMAN HEIMS	DARRELL R. PERRY
FRANK H. BAUER	LEON HEINZ	EDWARD PERREY
IRVING BEHLING	WALTER J. HENNING	PAUL POHLMAN
HARRY BERGMAN	GEORGE H. HERMANN	ALFRED POKEY
C. BENJAMIN BLOHM	CARL HERSCHLAG	ALBERT RASCHER
FRED BLOHM	RALPH HILDEBRANDT	REINHOLD B. REMUS
BENJAMIN BLUM	HENRY HINNEBERG	HENRY ROEHNER
LLOYD BRIGGS	A. GORDON HUMPHREY	WILLIAM SEINE
ALBERT CAVANAUGH	FRED W. HUNNEBERG	EDWIN SCHLINK
HENRY DAHLE	JAMES JENNINGS	LEON L. SCHMIDT
HOWARD P. DANIELS	WILLIAM KABLE	MARTIN SCHRAGE
BENJAMIN DEAN	CHARLES KLEIN	ALBERT C. SCHROLDIN
HERMAN C. DEVERMANN	HERMAN KNOCKE	ROBERT SCHULTZ
ALFRED DREYER	WALTER KRUEGER	HERMAN SCHWOLOW
BENJAMIN DREYER	WILLIAM KULZ	JOHN SCHWOLOW
OTTO DREYER	AUGUST LANGHOLF	JOHN STERNBERG
PAUL EBBESON	WALTER LARSON	JAMES S. STEWART
GEORGE FELL	JOHN LUERSSEN	FRED TEGTMEIR
WILLIAM FIEHN	WILLIAM H. MAIR	WILLIAM TOPPEL
MORTIMER FOSKET	FRED MAYER	LOUIS WAGNER
ROBERT FOSKET	WILLIAM MECHLENBERG	WILLIAM WERTH
FRANK V. FRASER	ARTHUR MESS	ERNST WIEHRDT
FRANK J. FREISE	WILLIAM MESS	PAUL D. WILSON
LESLIE FREYE	HENRY MOEHLING	ARTHUR WITT
ALEXANDER FUCHS	JAMES E. MORRIS, JR.	WALTER WITT
JOHN GAINER	SETH B. MORRIS	WILLIAM WITTENBERG
FRED HAEMKER, JR.	ROBERT H. MOSSER	BERNARD ZILLSDORF
FRED HARMENING	WALTER KUMMER	GEORGE ZIESHORE
FREDERICK HARMENING	LOUIS NERGE	
LEO HAWK	IRVING ROHDE	

This WW I Memorial was originally placed in the First National Bank, which closed its doors in 1932 during the bank crises of the Depression era. The plaque was placed on a stone at the flagpole and then moved to the entrance of the 1948 American Legion building at 122 West Palatine Road.

121

On August 19, 1919, Palatine held a homecoming parade to welcome its returned soldiers. There is no record of how this tank was obtained, but it was certainly an impressive feature of the day. Apparently, Palatine was very fond of its parades, or there was a major rivalry occurring, as you will see in the next photo.

On Saturday, September 27, 1919, the Palatine Welcome Home Celebration took place. It began with a street parade and pageant. These soldiers are marching in Hillside Cemetery either on this day or the August 19th parade. The day also featured an aeroplane exhibition, a band concert, dinner for all uniformed military people, and free dancing. "Soldier boys" of Schaumburg were guests of honor.

These gentlemen were part of the Selective Service System. They formed the Palatine Draft Board in 1941, and, in this picture, they are holding the lottery drawing for the draft. Some of the members are Bob Mosser (seated far right), E.P. Steinbrinck (seated with cigarette), George Howes (seated far left), Stuart Paddock (standing in back, left corner), Dr. Schmidke (standing in profile behind Mr. Steinbrinck), and George Wienecke (standing in the far left corner to Mr. Paddock's left) .

John O'Brien, at front row center, had been raised in Palatine by his grandparents, John and Hattie Umdenstock. O'Brien married a neighbor, Katherine Hans, the same day he received his draft notice. He was a bombardier on a B-24 bomber in New Guinea. On November 6, 1943, his plane was lost on a "milk run" and never recovered. He never saw his son, born in August of that year.

Dr. Carl D. Starck was the son of Dr. Carl A. Starck, who founded the Palatine Hospital. Capt. Starck served in the Army during WW II and sustained a compound fracture of his arm in a jeep accident in the Philippines. After the war, he was in family practice in Palatine.

This WW II Palatine Roll of Honor stood in the triangle that once held the Batterman Brick Building. Six hundred Palatine residents served in WW II. No one seems to know when the board was removed, but it was made of wood and fell apart. Since the late 1960s, the triangle has been occupied by the bank now named First Bank and Trust Co. of Illinois.

124

Harrison Kincaid married a Palatine girl, Maybelle Wenegar, in 1927. He received a commission as a lieutenant in the United States Army Reserve in 1925, the same year he graduated from college. He taught mathematics and science at Palatine High School and was one of the seven staff members in the new 1928 school. He was a basketball and track coach and, in 1930, the director of athletics. In 1931, he left Palatine High to teach at Crane Technical High School in Chicago. He was called out of the Reserves and into active duty as an instructor in 1943. He was stationed at Houston, Texas, teaching photography to bombardiers. He was discharged after the war as a major. Kincaid died suddenly on November 28, 1947, at his home at 303 North Hale Street.

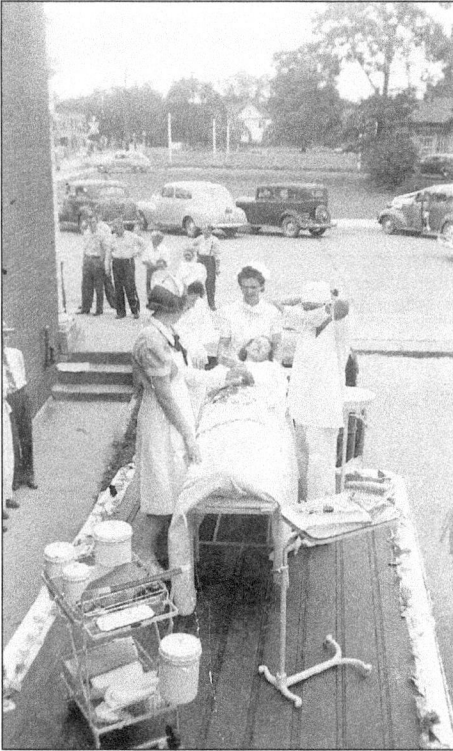

This is WW II on the home front. The Palatine Community Hospital nurses prepared this float in a local parade during the war. Camille Elliott stands at the side, and Vera Thorsen is at the head of the cart.

On Thursday, November 9, 1950, 20 Chicago and Northwestern freight cars piled up in the center of Palatine. Damage was primarily confined to railroad property, and no one was injured. Most of Palatine was without water for more than 24 hours. It took more than a week to clear the wreckage away. So many visitors poured into town over the weekend that state police were called in to handle traffic.

Palatine is not exactly in the tornado belt, although sometimes high winds cause damage. But in January 1960, a freak small tornado tore through Palatine and damaged display houses on East Palatine Road in the Winston Park subdivision. Some damage also occurred in the Palanois Park area, east of Northwest Highway.

A newspaper said of this snowstorm in February 1908: "It was the worst ever and the man was to be pitied who had to travel against that wind and blinding snow, with the thermometer below zero. William Daverman says last Saturday was the first time he ever failed to make a trip that he started upon." In recent years; 1967, 1979, and 1999; tremendous snowstorms have blown through the area.

Snowstorms are not uncommon in this part of the country, but an ice storm of this magnitude is seldom seen. This ice storm in the early 1960s caused a great deal of damage. On the right, electrical lines can be seen that have come down in the center of town. Some of the newer subdivisions were built with underground wiring.

The most tragic disaster in Palatine history occurred on February 23, 1973, when a fire destroyed the Ben Franklin Store. It cost the lives of three volunteer firemen: John Wilson, owner of the store; Warren Ahlgrim; and Richard Freeman. It was the beginning of the end for the volunteer fire department, leading to a full-time professional force.

www.ingramcontent.com/pod-product-compliance
Lightning Source LLC
Chambersburg PA
CBHW080904100426
42812CB00007B/2157